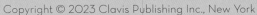

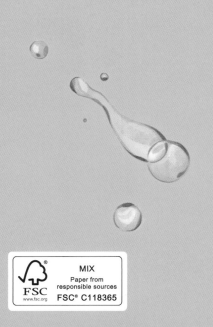

More titles in this series:

Builders
The Best Mommies and Daddies
The Largest
The Loudest

Copyright © 2023 Clavis Publishing Inc., New York

Originally published as *Superbeesjes. Reizigers*
in Belgium and the Netherlands by Clavis Uitgeverij, 2021
English translation from the Dutch by Clavis Publishing Inc., New York

Visit us on the Web at www.clavis-publishing.com.

Super Animals. Travelers written by Reina Ollivier and Karel Claes, and illustrated by Steffie Padmos

ISBN 978-1-60537-854-1

This book was printed in October 2022 at Nikara, M. R. Štefánika 858/25, 963 01 Krupina, Slovakia.

First Edition
10 9 8 7 6 5 4 3 2 1

Clavis Publishing supports the First Amendment and celebrates the right to read.

FSC
www.fsc.org
MIX
Paper from
responsible sources
FSC® C118365

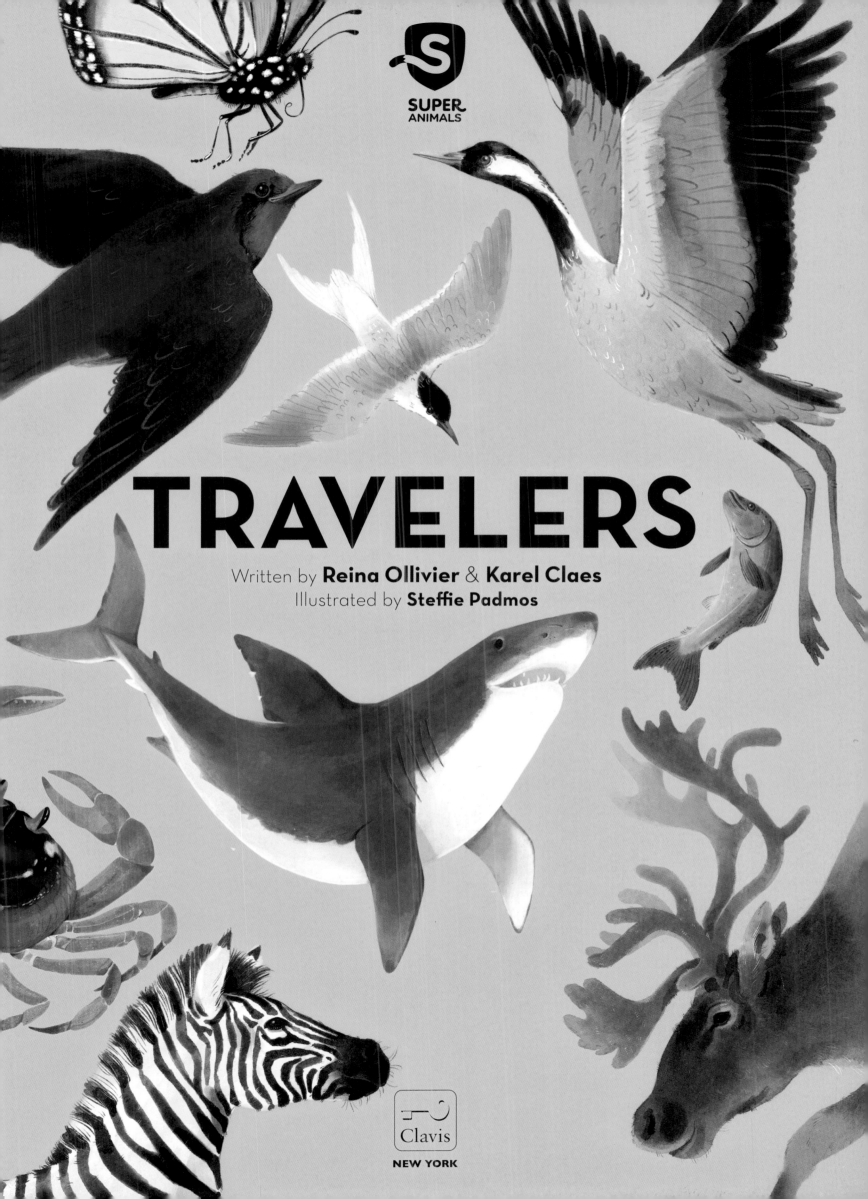

TRAVELERS

Written by **Reina Ollivier** & **Karel Claes**

Illustrated by **Steffie Padmos**

Clavis

NEW YORK

Dogs, cats, horses, cows, chickens . . .
are called domesticated animals.
Many of them are pets.
They're taken care of by people
and often live with them forever.

But there are also animals that are wild and travel.
Some live according to the seasons.
When there's no more food to be found,
they travel to another place, often far away.
Their instinct tells them where to go.
They don't need signs, maps, or computers. Isn't that cool?
Other animals take a long journey to lay eggs and reproduce.

In this book, we follow big and small travelers.
Which animal would you like to travel with?

CONTENTS

ARCTIC TERN

I'm a lightweight, but I achieve a gold medal as a traveler. I fly chasing the summer, from the top of the globe to the very bottom. This makes me the greatest traveler of all the animals on earth!

Who am I?

Name: Arctic tern
Class: birds

Legs:
2 short red legs

Size:
13 to 15 inches (33 to 39 centimeters) long

forked tail with 2 long **quills**

can **spread its tail feathers wide** to **hover** in midair

narrow, pointed wings with a wingspan of 26 to 30 inches (66 to 77 centimeters)

Habitat:
during the summer months along coasts, lakes, and swamps in the North; during the winter in the waters around the South Pole

Food:
fish, shrimp, crabs, krill, insects

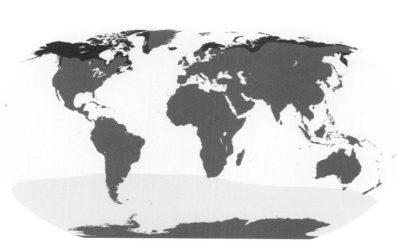

● breeding ground   ● wintering ground

Speed:
I can reach a top speed of 25 miles (40 kilometers) per hour.

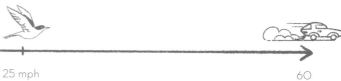

0   25 mph   60

Enemies:
They eat the eggs or the young of the Arctic tern.

 rats

 hedgehogs

 minks

 Arctic foxes

 polar bears

For my **nest** I use a **pit** in the ground. Because enemies can easily find this, we nest **in large groups** and help each other. I'm always ready to **defend** a nest. I attack the intruder from behind and dive for his head. I **keep attacking** and pecking with my beak **until he disappears.** This is how we also chase away **people and even polar bears** together!

weighs **only 3 to 4 ounces (90 to 120 grams)**

I'm **finely built** but **strong,** and I live to be over **30 years** old.

In the air I feel **my best,** and I shoot forward like an arrow. When I see something tasty, I **hover** over it for a moment and quickly flap my wings. From a height of almost **33 feet (10 meters),** I **drop on my prey.** Sometimes I dive **underwater** for food. I can **eat while flying** and even shout with a fish in my beak. Sometimes I'll **purposely startle** other birds and then steal the food they drop. If I **want to impress** a female, I give her a fish as a gift.

My **short legs** come in handy when I fly because I can completely retract them. But **on land** I'm very **clumsy.**

Traveler:
Every year the Arctic tern flies from the North Pole to the South Pole and back.

I love summer because there's a lot of food and it stays light outside for a long time. After breeding season, summer is over in the North, and the days get shorter. Time to leave! We gather in groups of around 15 birds. By the end of August, we fly to the South Pole. The seasons are reversed there: when I arrive in November, summer begins. So I fly from summer to summer!

Every year, we fly at least 25,000 miles (40,000 kilometers). Some birds wear radio devices that show they can fly 50,000 miles (80,000 kilometers). That's two trips around the globe!

The journey south takes 3 months, with a few stops in between to eat and rest. The return trip back north is much faster: only 40 days. We leave in March and are back at our nesting place by April or May. Usually, we return to the same place.

Heading south, we fly along the African or South American coast. On the return trip, we're led by a strong tailwind. We fly in an S-shape over the Atlantic Ocean, alternately along Africa and South America.

CHINOOK SALMON

My name refers to the area where the Chinook, a group of Native Americans, lived. Nowadays you can find Chinook salmon in many other places. On my first trip, I swim with the current. My last trip is upstream and takes me back to where it all began.

Who am I?

Name: Chinook salmon
Class: fish

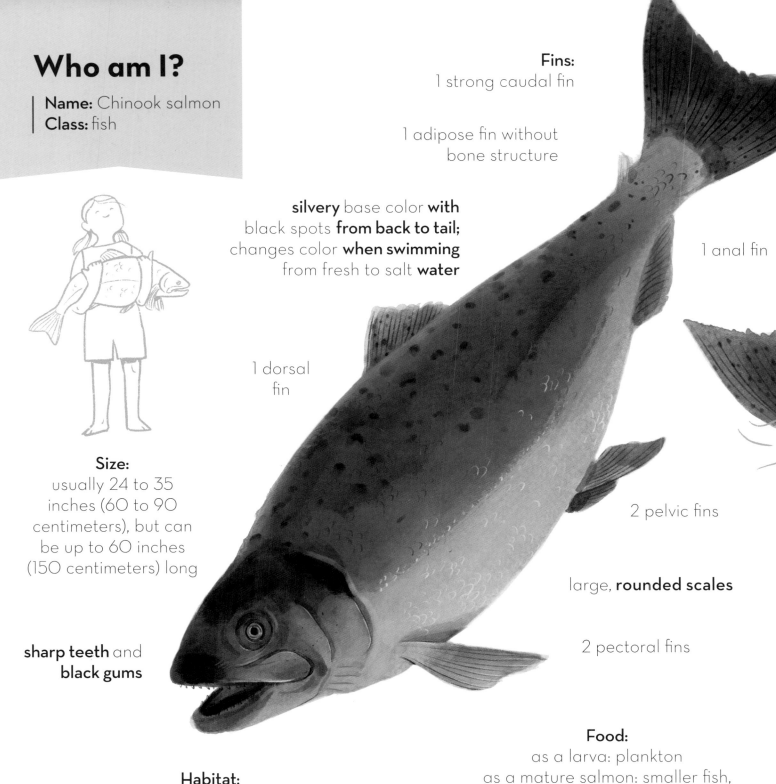

Fins:
1 strong caudal fin

1 adipose fin without bone structure

1 anal fin

silvery base color **with** black spots **from back to tail;** changes color **when swimming** from fresh to salt **water**

1 dorsal fin

Size:
usually 24 to 35 inches (60 to 90 centimeters), but can be up to 60 inches (150 centimeters) long

2 pelvic fins

large, **rounded scales**

2 pectoral fins

sharp teeth and **black gums**

Food:
as a larva: plankton
as a mature salmon: smaller fish, squid, small crabs, and lobsters

Habitat:
seas and rivers in America, Asia, and New Zealand; also released into lakes for breeding

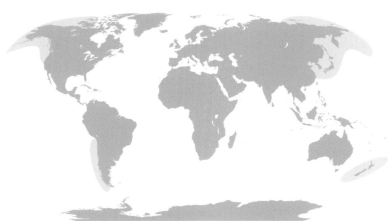

Speed:
I swim around 8 miles (13 kilometers) per hour.

0   8 mph   100

Enemies:
The biggest enemies are fishermen.

| fishermen | bigger fish | killer whales | humpback whales | seals | eagles | bears | otters |

Of all the salmon species, I'm **the largest,** which is why I'm also called **king salmon** in America. I sometimes weigh more than **120 pounds (55 kilograms)!** I like **pure and oxygenated water** with a temperature of 50 to 57 degrees Fahrenheit (10 to 14 degrees Celsius).

My **biggest enemy** are **fishermen,** who try to catch me everywhere. I'm a **wild salmon** and swim freely in nature. Some Chinook salmon are **bred in cages** in the sea.

Traveler:
The Chinook salmon swims from its birthplace in the river to the ocean, and at the end of its life it swims back to its birthplace.

I come **from an egg in fresh water** but spend **most years** of my life in the **salt water** of the sea. When the time comes to **breed, I return** to my freshwater home. I choose a spot at the bottom of the river where there are many **pebbles.** I make a **pit** in them with my fins and my tail. I lay **hundreds of eggs,** which are immediately **fertilized** by a male. With a sweep of my tail, I wipe pebbles over the fertilized eggs to **protect** them. I make a **new pit,** and the **male follows.** We continue like that until the last of my **4,000 to 5,000 eggs** are laid. The male and I **die** before the eggs hatch.

I stay near my hometown for a year. It's 1,850
miles (3,000 kilometers) away from the ocean.
From a small larva, I grow into a young fish
of 6 inches (15 centimeters) in length.
Then I leave on a journey down
the river. I have to watch out
for bigger fish or birds
that want to eat me.

When I'm between
2 and 6 years old,
I swim by myself,
deep in the ocean.
I have a huge appetite
and grow into a giant fish.
Then it'll be time for my
final journey home. I'll swim
the nearly 1,850 miles (3,000
kilometers) upstream without
eating anymore. It's a difficult
and dangerous journey, with many
changes in elevation. Sometimes I have
to pass a dam or go through warmer water
or polluted areas. At a waterfall, I throw myself
into the air and try to get higher. Bears, otters,
eagles, and people want to catch me. I reach my
final destination exhausted, full of scratches and
wounds. Many salmon don't survive this journey.

Along the way, I eat a lot and grow rapidly.
I swim thousands of miles to where the river
flows into the ocean. My first big journey ends
here. In this area mixed with fresh and salt
water, I meet other young Chinook salmon.

Our bodies adapt so we
can live in salt water.
Then we swim out to sea.

PLAINS ZEBRA

During my search for food and water, I follow the seasons. I always move clockwise. This way, I travel back in a big circle to the area where I came from.

Who am I?

Name: plains zebra
Class: mammals

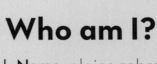

stripes running **down** the body; at the **buttocks and legs** the stripes are **horizontal**

the **only zebra species** with **stripes on the belly;** the belly of other zebras is white

Size:
4 to 4.6 feet (1.20 to 1.40 meters) shoulder height and 6.5 to 8 feet (about 2 to 2.50 meters) long

large ears that can turn in almost all directions

tassel on the tail

Legs:
4 long legs, each with 1 large hoof, like a horse

short, stiff upright **mane**

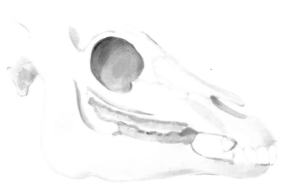

sharp incisors to cut grass and **large molars** at the back to grind that grass; they wear down but always keep growing

Habitat:
grassy areas in Central and South Africa, with trees or bushes here and there

Food:
mainly grass, also leaves, small twigs, bark

Speed:
I reach a top speed of 40 miles (65 kilometers) per hour.

0   40 mph   60

Enemies:

 lions
 leopards
 hyenas
 cheetahs
 wild dogs
 crocodiles

I live in a **family with one male,** a few other females, and several foals. We regularly join **zebra families** that we meet. This is **safer,** because we have to watch out for attackers day and night. We **sleep standing up.**

Lions in particular hunt us. They sneak up on us and try to surprise us. There's always a strong **zebra on guard,** and he warns us if he sees or smells lions. Then we all sprint away. If a lion does come too close, I give him a **powerful backward kick** with my hooves.

My **foal** recognizes me by my **smell** and my **stripes.** The stripes are different on each zebra. I'm actually a **black zebra with white stripes,** because the skin under my coat is dark.

Traveler:
The plains zebra travels hundreds of miles each year to find food and water.

Our **striped pattern** is quite **useful.** The alternation between white and black **confuses** stinging **insects,** so I get stung less. When our herd runs away, a **lion** has trouble seeing where one zebra begins and another one ends. As a result, he can't **calculate his jump properly.**

23

I eat a lot of dry grass, and I need to drink enough to wash that down. But where I live in Africa, there isn't always water or food. I migrate from grazing areas in the dry season to grazing areas in the rainy season. That's why I don't have a permanent home; I'm always on the move.

I travel around 300 miles (500 kilometers) a year. When I move, I don't walk; I trot. I can't lose time, because I have to graze for 7 hours every day to get enough food. I move fast and can maintain that speed for a very long time.

Along the way, wildebeests often move with our zebra families. Antelopes, ostriches, and giraffes also like to stay near us.

Together we form impressive herds of thousands of animals. We're loved by our fellow travelers because we can hear well and see far, even at night. That way, we notice enemies more quickly. Crossing rivers is especially dangerous because crocodiles are lurking there to catch us.

RED CRAB

I live alone in my little hole in the rain forest, but in November I go out with millions of others at a time and crawl to the sea like a living river. Once I've mated with a female, I return to my own place.

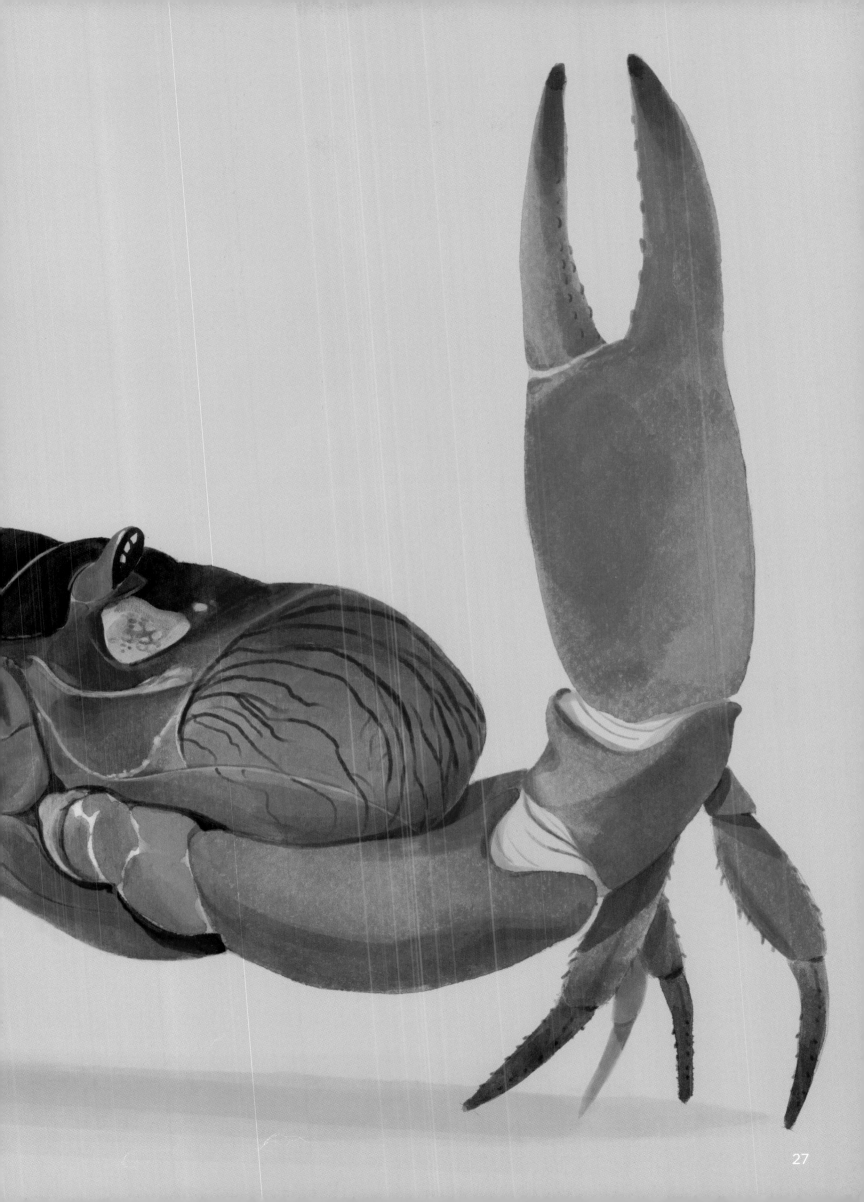

Who am I?

Name: red crab
Class: crustaceans

Legs:
8 walking legs,
and 2 forelegs
with pincers

Size:
shell is 4 to 5 inches (11
to 12 centimeters) wide;
females are smaller

Habitat:
damp, shady spots on Christmas
Island in the Indian Ocean

Food:
Adult crabs eat leaves, fruit,
flowers, seedlings, giant African
snails, and dead red crabs.

Speed:
I travel just under a mile
(1.50 kilometers) a day.

0 <1 mile a day

Enemies:
Larvae hatching from eggs are eaten by:

manta rays   fish   whale sharks

Adult crabs are eaten by:

yellow crazy ants

if a **pincer** is **torn off,** a **new one** grows back, but it stays **smaller**

Traveler:
The red crab migrates annually from the rain forest to the coast to mate.

My **shell grows slowly,** and only after 4 years is it 5.5 inches (14 centimeters) wide. Every time my body gets **too big, I shed the shell** and a new one grows back. Now that I'm an adult, this only happens once a year. I can live to be **20 to 30 years old.**

brown marking on the **back;** the left and right side are each other's mirror image

I like a **humid environment,** so I choose a place to live in the **rain forest.** With my hind legs I **dig** out earth. At the front, I push it away with my pincers. This way, I make a **tunnel** to my **little house under the ground,** which has one room. I live by myself, but there are 44 million crabs on the island, each in its own little hole.

In the **dry season** it gets way **too hot,** and I don't come out for 2 or 3 months. I **close off** my **tunnel** with a wad of **wet leaves,** so it stays delightfully damp in the house.

During the first storm of the rainy season, I take a trip to the coast. I cover a distance of 2.5 miles (4 kilometers). That takes me about a week. If the rainy season starts early, I have plenty of time. If the rainy season is late, I have to hurry.

I'm a male, and we leave first because we're digging breeding holes at the ocean for females. I travel early in the morning or late in the afternoon when it's cooler. If I walk for too long in the blazing sun, I dehydrate and die.

We crawl on and under everything and don't let anything stop us. Because many crabs have been run over by cars during this trip, people have built tunnels for us. And even a crab bridge!

When I arrive at the ocean, I immediately dive into the water to replenish my liquid supply. Then I start digging. Sometimes another male wants to take my hole and we fight. After mating with a female, I replenish my liquid supply in the ocean again. I return home, and the female stays behind. The eggs develop in her brood pouch. When the moon is in the right position (the last quarter), she releases the eggs into the ocean. She does this at high tide, so that the retreating water takes the eggs with it. Then she also travels back to her hole in the rain forest.

BARN SWALLOW

As you can guess, I love farming areas. I find building materials for my nest there and an abundance of food. There's plenty of space and also water nearby. I take a long trip twice a year.

Who am I?

Name: barn swallow
Class: birds

Legs:
2 short legs with few muscles because the barn swallow mostly flies and rests little

long and narrow wings with a wingspan of 11.5 to 12.5 inches (29 to 32 centimeters)

Size:
6 to 7.5 inches (15 to 19 centimeters) long

short, broad beak; reddish-brown spot below and above the beak

forked tail with **long, thin tips** to turn quickly in the air; females have shorter tail tips

Habitat:
in built-on areas near water in Europe, Africa, America, Asia, and Oceania

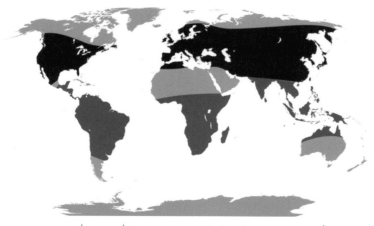

• summer breeding ground   • wintering ground

Food:
all kinds of flying insects, especially mosquitoes; also beetles, alates, butterflies, wasps, bees, and aphids

Speed:
I fly about 25 miles (40 kilometers) per hour on my long journey, but when I swoop, I go much faster.

0   25 mph   60

Enemies:

falcons gulls snakes martens lynxes

Traveler:
The barn swallow flies south in late summer and returns in spring.

I usually live **near people.** I prefer to choose a spot in the **barn or stable** of a farm. There we can fly in and out undisturbed. But barns and stables are becoming more closed off. Therefore, my female and I now often build the nest **under a canopy or bridge.** We apply **clumps of mud** and glue them together with saliva. We reinforce our nest with **grass or straw.** Inside we put soft **feathers.** It's nice for our young. I'm small, but I **defend** our **nest** bravely by attacking intruders.

During the day, I fly almost all the time and catch **thousands of mosquitoes.** You often see me whizzing closely **over water** because there are lots of mosquitoes there. In between, I scoop up some water with my beak to **drink.** Thanks to my long, narrow tail and wings, I **quickly change direction and height.** I'm a real acrobat!

Outside the breeding season, I like to be with other barn swallows. We sometimes roost **in large groups** on power lines, fences, or reed stems. We warn each other when there's **danger,** but we also regularly **quarrel** and fight for the best sleeping place.

35

When our last hatchlings mature, it gets colder. In September, we leave our nests and gather by the thousands. We eat extra to be strong for the long journey.

I leave for the South because there are few insects here in the winter. We travel in large swarms and protect each other from enemies. I use up a lot of strength along the way, because I fly about 250 miles (400 kilometers) a day. Every few days, I take a rest day. I do fly around for a few hours then to catch insects.

I fly over 5,000 miles (8,000 kilometers) from Europe to Africa, where I spend the winter. If it gets too hot there, I know that spring is coming up north. I fly back on the same path to my old nest.

People are always happy when
they see me return from my trip.
They say I bring spring, sunshine,
and warmth.

GREAT WHITE SHARK

Only my stomach is white; the rest of my body is gray.
I'm happy with that because that way, I don't stand out
in the water and I can attack unexpectedly. I not only
travel far but also deep into the ocean.

Who am I?

Name: great white shark
Class: fish

Fins:
1 high dorsal fin

streamlined and **strong muscular** body; can therefore swim **quickly** in all directions

Size:
13 to 20 feet (4 to 6 meters) long; females are bigger than males

an upright tail in the shape of a crescent moon

1 small dorsal fin

2 long pectoral fins

2 short pelvic fins

1 anal fin

Habitat:
in all the cool but not too cold waters of the oceans; often not far from the coast, where the water is less than 1 mile (1.50 kilometers) deep

Food:

mackerel, tuna, seals, dolphins, sea lions, elephant seals, young whales, small sharks

Speed:
I swim 15.5 miles (25 kilometers) per hour, with top speeds up to 25 miles (40 kilometers) per hour.

0   25 mph   60

Traveler:
The great white shark dives very deep and swims thousands of miles back and forth each year.

humans

pointed snout with wide, slightly **receding mouth**

around 300 **triangular teeth,** 3 inches (7 centimeters) long, in **several rows;** replaced when they fall out or break off

5 **gill slits** for breathing; these take in **oxygen** from the water entering the mouth

When I hunt, I try to **surprise** my **prey.** I swim under the animal, swing my body up at lightning speed, and bite. I can jump out of the water up to 10 feet (3 meters). After my first bite, I release and wait for the **prey** to **weaken** to start my meal.

I have very **good eyes** and a **fantastic nose.** Underwater I can smell a group of seals from miles away. This allows me to look for **food even in the dark.**

I usually **hunt by myself,** but other white sharks sometimes eat with me because they **smell** the **blood** of my prey from afar. We're also good **cleaners.** If a whale dies, we often go after it with several other sharks. We **eat everything,** so there's nothing left.

Human flesh isn't on my menu. **Attacking** a **human** is usually done **by mistake** or out of curiosity.

As a young shark, I swam in shallow coastal waters for several years, eating mostly fish. Now that I'm an adult, I dive over half a mile (1,000 meters) deep. And I can't do that near the coast.

In the depths, the water is colder. The fish there have less energy and therefore swim much slower. I can keep warm better than they can and don't lose strength. Therefore, I can easily find prey there.

Meanwhile, I also eat larger animals like seals and sea lions. I know exactly where and when they have young. Every year I take a trip of about 2,500 miles (4,000 kilometers) to the best places with the most food.

During that long journey I swim through open oceans where I can't find food. But that's no problem, because then I live off my fat reserves. I can go without food for a long time. When I arrive at a hunting ground, I replenish my fat reserves. It feels good to stuff myself then.

COMMON CRANE

In the fall I can't find enough food up north, where I live. So, I spread my big wings and fly in groups to the South. Even as a young bird, I flew with my parents.

Who am I?

Name: common crane
Class: birds

Size:
43 to 47 inches
(110 to 120
centimeters) tall

Legs:
2 slender
legs, each
with 3 long
toes

red eyes and
red spot on
the crown

wingspan 6.5 to 8 feet
(2 to 2.45 meters)

long neck, fully
stretched when flying

Habitat:
breeding in wetlands and swamps in
northern Europe and northern Asia; hibernating
in southern Europe, northern or eastern Africa,
the Middle East, India, or southern China

Food:
omnivore: plants, grass roots,
leaves, berries, acorns, grains,
insects, snails, worms, lizards, frogs,
salamanders, toads, small mammals,
fish, small birds, eggs

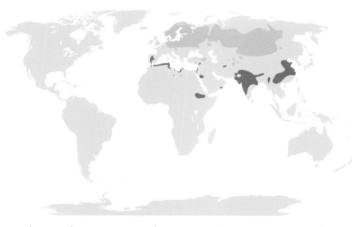

● breeding ground ● wintering ground

Speed:
Over water, I fly up to 45 miles
(70 kilometers) per hour, but
over land, only 25 miles
(40 kilometers) per hour.

0   45 mph   100

Enemies:

hunters

foxes

bears

eagles

power lines

short tail with the **large feathers** of the wings hanging over it

I spend **most of the day** looking for **food.** I carefully walk through the water or on land with my **long legs.** I'm **easily scared** and constantly look around me. At the slightest threat, I fly away.

When I find a **partner,** we perform a **dance** together. We take short steps around each other with our wings half open. At the same time, we bend and stretch our legs and our necks. Occasionally, we jump up and fan our wings. We **trumpet** loudly and from then on **always** stay **together.**

We build our **nest** on a small **rise in the water.** Our **chicks grow quickly** and leave the nest before they can fly. They chase us into the swamp, where they're safer from attackers.

I can live to be **30 years old,** and in many countries, they say common cranes bring **good luck.** Have you ever folded a common crane out of paper?

47

Starting in late August, I look for other common cranes. We eat a lot, and our bodies adapt. Our hearts enlarge, and our chest muscles become firmer. This is important, because we're taking a trip of at least 2,500 miles (4,000 kilometers)!

During the flight, we fly in a V-shape and take turns leading. Those who fly behind the leader can rest a bit. We keep our legs and necks stretched. Occasionally, we float along on warm air currents and rest our wings. We trumpet so loudly that you can hear us coming from 3 miles (5 kilometers) away.

Along the way, we rest for a few days. We then spend the night in shallow water and early in the morning fly to newly harvested fields nearby. Especially on stubble fields of corn, we find lots of food. In the evening, we return in groups. The other common cranes welcome us with trumpeting, and we answer their greeting. At our regular stops, we sometimes troop together with 80,000 common cranes!

As soon as we've regained enough strength, we fly on toward the place where we spend the winter. In our favorite area, we're usually with more than 120,000 other common cranes.

CARIBOU

I live in the wild, but some people keep reindeer as pets. I feel best in cold areas. I don't like to be alone, and I travel in large herds. In some countries, they call me a reindeer.

Who am I?

Name: caribou
Class: mammals

Size:
4 to 5 feet (1.20 to 1.50 meters) shoulder height and 5 to 7 feet (1.60 to 2.10 meters) long; females are smaller

broad hooves
give them a good
grip in deep snow

Legs:
4 strong legs, each with 2 deeply split front hooves and 2 long side hooves

antlers up to 3 feet (1 meter) wide; in males up to almost 5 feet (1.50 meters) long with many branches; in females only up to 1.5 feet (50 centimeters) long. Every year, the old one falls off, and a new and larger antler grows in spring.

eyes adapt during the dark winter period, so that they **see** better **in low light**

Food:
during winter, lichen; when the snow has disappeared, also grass, leaves, young branches, berries, and mushrooms

Habitat:
cold areas of northern America, Europe, and Asia

Speed:
I run an average of 7.5 miles (12 kilometers) per hour, but I can reach a top speed of 45 miles (70 kilometers) per hour.

0   45 mph   60

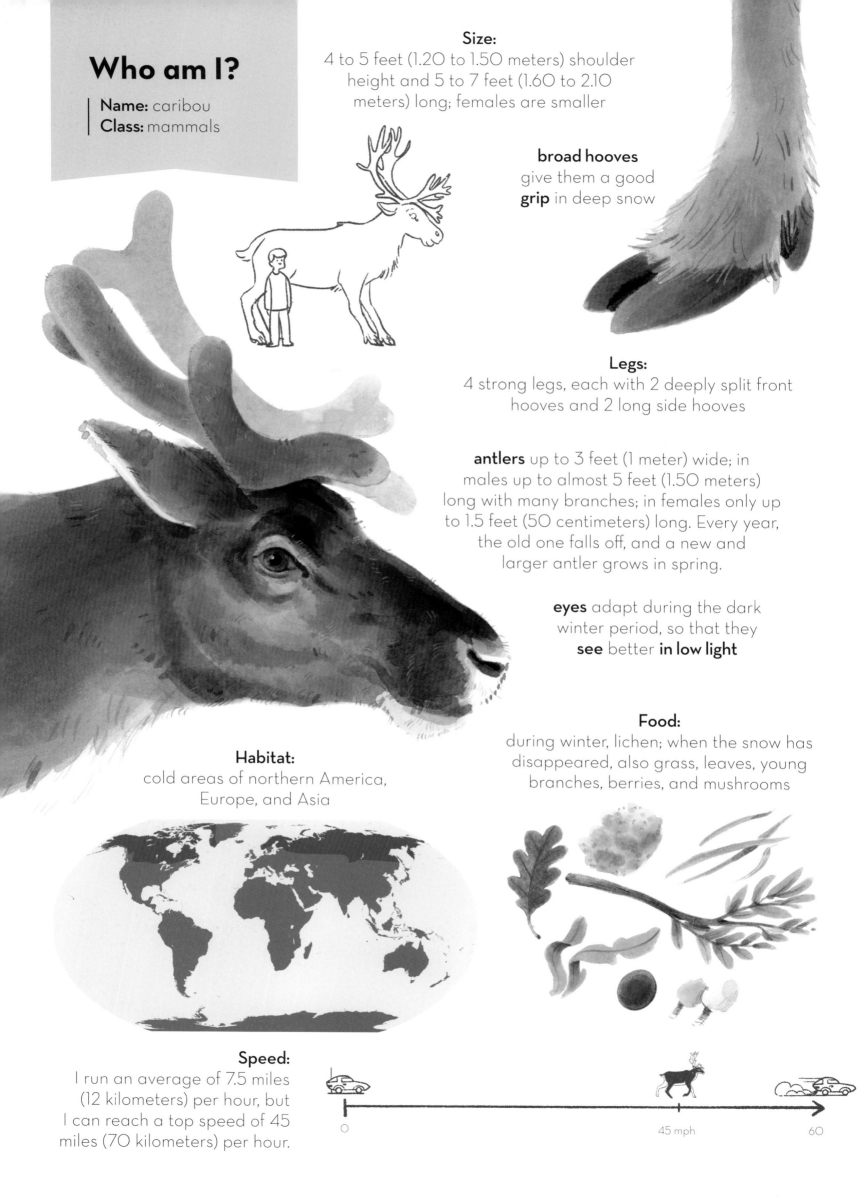

Enemies:

wolves   bears   lynxes   other stinging and
biting insects

Traveler:
The caribou migrates year-round in search of food and in winter travels thousands of miles south, where it's a little less cold.

hairy tail that's 4 to 10 inches (10 to 25 centimeters) long

We're the **only animals** in the **deer family** in which **females** have **antlers.** The males lose their antlers in the fall. I'm a female and don't lose my antlers until after winter because I have to take care of my **calf.** With my **delicate nose,** I can smell **lichen** under 1.5 feet (50 centimeters) of snow. I scrape away the snow with my hooves so the calf can reach the moss. If a male wants to eat it, I chase him away with my antlers.

Sometimes it gets **60 degrees below zero Fahrenheit (50 degrees below zero Celsius).** That doesn't bother me because my **coat** consists of two layers. I have a soft coat underneath and above that a thick outer coat with hollow hairs. Those **hollow hairs** are full of air and **protect** me **from the cold.** In **summer,** my coat is **grayish brown.** In **winter,** it turns **white,** so I don't stand out too much in the snow.

Some areas are home to **domesticated reindeer.** People keep them for their **meat, milk, and butter.** Those reindeer **pull sleds** and carry loads of up to 285 pounds (130 kilograms). Their **hides** are made into **warm clothing,** shoes, and blankets. The **antlers** are made into **utensils or art.**

From June, we're plagued by swarms of **mosquitoes and other biting insects.** They're not only **annoying** but suck our blood and can greatly **weaken** the **herd.**

I'm a real wanderer and never stay in the same place for long. Even my calf can walk with our herd of thousands of animals just a few hours after being born.

In the fall, we take a big trip south because there's nothing left to eat up north. We travel about 34 miles (55 kilometers) every day and sometimes end up more than 1,250 miles (2,000 kilometers) farther south. It's warmer there or, more accurately, less cold. It's still freezing cold, and there's snow everywhere.

During the migration, we swim through lakes and rivers. The hollow hairs of our fur keep us afloat, a bit like a floatie. And we spread our hooves wide like flippers, so that we can paddle smoothly through the water. We reach speeds of 6 to 12 miles (10 to 20 kilometers) per hour. A herd of swimming reindeer is an impressive sight!

Together with the other females, I lead everyone back to the grassy plains up north in the spring. By then, there'll be lots of fresh greens again!

MONARCH BUTTERFLY

I was born in the North of America and fly all the way south, where my ancestors are from. And I do so without anyone showing me the way!

Who am I?

Name: monarch butterfly
Class: insects

Legs:
3 pairs of legs

wingspan of 3 to 4 inches
(7 to 10 centimeters)

2 pairs of wings;
black wing
margin, dotted
with white dots

Size:
2 inches
(5 centimeters)
long; males larger
than females

2 thin
antennae,
each with
a **button** at
the end

rolling tongue to suck nectar from flowers

front 2 **legs** are **shorter**
and serve to brush antennae

4 **other legs** have
claws for catching
on to things

Food:
Caterpillars eat only leaves of
silk plants. Butterflies suck nectar
from all kinds of flowers.

Habitat:
in warm areas where silk plants grow in
America, islands in the Pacific and
Atlantic oceans, and in southern Spain

Speed:
I reach a top speed of 11 miles
(18 kilometers) per hour and
even more if I get carried
away by strong winds.

0   11 mph   60

Enemies:

Eggs are eaten by:

predatory mites

small insects

Caterpillars and butterflies are eaten by:

birds

insects

spiders

centipedes

mice

My life began in an **egg** on a **silk plant.** I crawled out as a tiny quarter-inch (6-millimeter) **larva** and grew into a 2-inch (45-millimeter) **striped caterpillar.** I spun myself into a cocoon called a **chrysalis.** In it, I **gradually** changed into a **butterfly.**

Traveler:
Only the monarch butterflies from North America make the long journey south.

As a caterpillar, I ate **poisonous plants** and stored that poison in my body. As a butterfly, I still have that poison, and that's why some **birds don't eat me.**

My **wings** are quite **large** for a butterfly. With a few beats of my wings, I can let myself **drift on the wind.** I don't have to flutter very often. The **veins** in my wings give me extra **strength.** Females have thicker veins than males.

The strange habits of **humans threaten** my life. They use poisons in nature and cut down the trees in which I hibernate. The **warming climate confuses** me, and I'm not sure when to leave anymore. There are also **fewer silk plants** growing, and I can only lay my **eggs** on those plants.

I live in a flat area east of the Rocky Mountains, a large mountain range in North America. In the fall, it gets colder and I float south along on warm air currents. I'm a diurnal butterfly (meaning I'm active during the day), and during my trip, I sleep in trees at night. In 2 months' time, I travel all the way to Mexico, almost 2,750 miles (4,500 kilometers) away. But I'm not alone. Millions of monarch butterflies make the same journey.

The monarch butterflies on the west side of the Rocky Mountains don't travel as far. They fly to the forests near the coast of California.

In Mexico, I join other groups of monarch butterflies. We find a spot in our favorite tree: the sacred silver fir. We huddle close together for warmth and hardly move until winter is over. I'm very light (about the weight of a piece of gum!), but when we hang by tens of thousands on a branch, it can break off.

In March, I travel north again. I lay eggs and will die on the way. The butterflies from those eggs fly farther north. They don't live as long as I do: only 5 to 7 weeks. From their eggs, new butterflies grow and continue their journey. After the third or fourth group of eggs, the monarch butterflies end up in the North at the end of summer. Those butterflies become distance travelers like me and live for 8 months.

**Have a safe trip,
and be careful!**